THE

SOURCE

Putting God Back on the Throne

Kierston S. Lewis

Printed in the United States of America

Keen Vision Publishing, LLC
www.keen-vision.com
ISBN: 978-1-948270-54-0

Dedicated To YOU...

CONTENTS

THE SOURCE

Through life testimonies and spiritual revelations, you'll begin to witness the miraculous, delivering power of God. God is the source of all we need, and once we understand this, we can walk boldly knowing that we are not living this life alone. Often times, we put things in our lives above God, subconsciously, thinking and believing that we know what is best for ourselves. However, once you begin to bare witness to the unwavering favor and unconditional love of God you will never want to live the same again. The Source will challenge you to reevaluate your life. It will empower you to embrace the perspective of God. Most of all, The Source will encourage you to keep living! There is more to life than what you have experienced, but have you been pulling from the right source?

Section One

FIX YOUR
SOURCE

Chapter One

ADDICTION

"Dear brothers and sisters, if another believer is overcome by some sin, you who are godly should gently and humbly help that person back onto the right path. And be careful not to fall into the same temptation yourself. Share each other's burdens, and in this way obey the law of Christ."

Galatians 6:1-2 (NLT)

As believers, we will always be tempted to place things in our lives above God. Pornography was my first temptation. At the age of 13, I was exposed to it in a computer lab at my school. One of my classmates went to a website and played a video of two people having sex for the entire class to see. As the video played, some of the students laughed and made jokes. Others, like me, just stood there in complete shock. I never fathomed that I would become addicted to pornography years later. After all, it started as a joke.

After that day, I became curious. My porn addiction started very subtly, just a little 'research' here and there. Little did I know, the curse that had plagued my bloodline for generations had now manifested in me. One day, as I was casually 'researching' on my laptop, I heard my mom call for me.

"Can I see your computer?" she asked. Ignorant of how to clear my browser history, I just exited out of the site and gave it to her. Shortly after, she called me into her room. With disgust on her face, she asks me these three dreaded words:

"What is this?"

How do you explain a browser history full of pornography to your mother? What can you say after being caught? I was scared out of my mind and tried my best to climb out of a hole that I put myself in. My explanations only made things worse. I almost collapsed to the floor when she threatened to tell my dad. At the time, it seemed like the worse idea ever. However, as I look back, I wish she would have told my dad. I wish someone would have explained to me the dangers of having a porn addiction.

Throughout college, I began watching porn for different reasons, primarily coping. Every student dealt with the stresses of college differently. Some drank. Some smoked. Some had sex. I was never a heavy drinker, never had the desire to smoke, and I was still a virgin. So in my mind, I figured that I would be the last person in line to hell for satisfying my sexual desires through porn. I sought the theological stand-point of masturbation for a long time. I genuinely wanted to know if it was truly a sin because I had never seen it spoken of, specifically, in the Bible. So since I didn't understand the biblical context of it, nor did I receive language for it in the church, I followed the advice of my peers. They told me things like,

"There's nothing wrong with it."
"It's natural!"
"It helps relieve stress."
"I do it sometimes, too."

But no one could explain why I felt so depressed, empty, and ashamed afterward. Everyone hyped and glorified the pleasurable parts of pornography and masturbation but no one mentioned the painful decline from the cyclical high. After I satisfied my itch, I felt disgusted looking at the very thing that gave me pleasure. No one could explain why. So, what else was I to do? As a young adult, who else could I have talked to about this touchy subject? I was too ashamed and prideful to take it before God. So, I conformed, and pornography and masturbation became my source.

> "Your eye is like a lamp that provides light to your body. When your eye is healthy, your whole body is filled with light. But when your eye is unhealthy, your whole body is filled with darkness. And if the light you think you have is actually darkness, how deep that darkness is!"
>
> Matthew 6:22-23 NLT

I became a slave to my urges, and instead of talking about it, I suffered in silence. Every other Sunday, I found myself at the altar secretly begging to be free. That was until the church that I had attended discontinued the ministry (continuation in Chapter Two). Upon partnering with a new age church a few months later, it was as if the blinders fell off of my eyes. For once, I felt the help that I needed had finally come. Then, I knew that I was not alone!

As I attended one of the church services, I will never forget the level of deliverance that we experienced that day. We all began to lay our devices of addiction on the altar. Pills, Condoms, Cigarettes, Weed, Liquor Bottles, Lighters, Cell Phones! It blew me away. I came to the realization, "God, if you can still love them even in their situation, maybe you can help me after all." After that day, I openly declared and made a decision that I did not want this life anymore. I went into my closet and closed the door. I didn't cry, whine, or moan. I just laid there and told God everything. I verbally confessed every detail, from start to finish, of how I became addicted to porn and masturbation. I refused to withhold anything else from him. I was serious about my freedom. Of course, he already knew the details, but I chose to soften my heart and freely give it to him. I didn't get completely free from pornography and masturbation that same day. I still slipped back into the temptation, but God lovingly helped me back up every time.

The frequency of my urges changed from every day to every other day to every other week to every other month. Soon enough, I did not have the desire to partake in it at all anymore. I was free.

Freedom is a process, but it starts with making a DAILY decision to stay free! With every declaration and every 'no,' God works on our hearts and changes our desires. When he becomes our source, we will never feel like we are fighting alone. He will always be there to catch us, and in his safety, we gain the strength necessary to change.

REVELATION

A child wanders away from supervision with no warning of the dangers that he may face. His friends encourage him to do dangerous things. They said it would be fun, but the child gets hurt. Upon this happening, his friends were nowhere to be found. Yet in the midst of his lonesome, he calls his Father. Once they get home, he tells his Father everything that led to the fall. The Father embraces him and tells him that everything is going to be okay. Throughout the healing process, the child was very limited, so he had to depend on his Father for even the things he could normally do by himself. The Father was there to catch the child every time he slipped and tripped. He healed much quicker in the arms of the Father than he would have alone.

> "But you belong to God, my dear children. You have already won a victory over those people, because the Spirit who lives in you is greater than the spirit who lives in the world."
>
> 1 John 4:4 NLT

Chapter Two

CHURCH HURT

"We are made right with God by placing our faith in Jesus Christ. And this is true for everyone who believes, no matter who we are. For everyone has sinned; we all fall short of God's glorious standard. Yet, God, in his grace, freely makes us right in his sight. He did this through Christ Jesus when he freed us from the penalty for our sins."

Romans 3:22-24 (NLT)

L et's debunk a very common myth that even I had believed for some time: Church hurt is not real. I had to come to the hard reality that the church did not hurt me; my expectations of people did. Biblically, the church was set aside as the bride of Christ (Ephesians 5:23-27).

The church was signified as holy, clean, washed with the word of God, and without spot, wrinkle or any other blemish. It's very irrational and dangerous for us to hold accusations of church hurt against the entirety of the church — God's bride. Despite what transpires within the body of Christ and among the people of God, the aspiration of the church has always been to be holy, clean, washed with the word of God, and without spot, wrinkle or any other blemish.

As believers, we must be cautious of the pedestals we put people on. We have a terrible habit of withdrawing from God because of the mistakes of a leader (or a person whom we hold to a high standard). We should never put so much hope and trust in people that when they mess up, we turn away from God. That was never his intent for us.

All people that proclaim the name of Christ are expected to live a righteous life — not JUST the leaders. In our humanity, God knew that we would always need his grace, thus he sent his son to die on the cross for our future mistakes. So if God, in all of his sovereignty, decides to grant us grace, nothing should disqualify us from giving that same grace to others — even those who stand on the platform!

We must come to the resolve that the church, God's bride, did not hurt us. If we think about the last painful encounter we experienced in the church, there was always an ungodly spirit attached to and fueling it, i.e., Jezebel, pride, divination, corruption, greed, and Pharisee. You may be thinking, "Kierston, what makes you credible to give this information? What qualifies you to tell us this?" The 'church hurt' that I faced carried the majority of these spirits. As a result of making my leader the source of my relationship with God, I almost left the church for good after the ministry hit the fan.

At 18, I moved to north Alabama to attend college. Honestly, I was not thinking about church at all because of my upbringing. Serving as the choir director's granddaughter was just as demanding as being a preacher's kid, in my opinion. I grew up in the same church and sang in the same choir for well over 13 years, and I can count on one hand how many Sundays I missed. When I moved, I decided that I would leave church behind. In my eyes, 13 years of serving the church were enough. Nevertheless, upon my arrival at college, I received a call from my cousin telling me that she was going to pick me up for church that weekend.

Within the first year of attending a new church, I began serving just as I did at my home church. I was singing on the praise and worship team, but still living in my dysfunction.

There I was, serving and sinning, repenting and repeating. I knew that God loved me, and he would always forgive me. So I lived the sinner's dream. What I failed to take into account were the principles of God. Yes, he loves me. Yes, he forgave me, but it would surely come to pass that whatever I sowed into the earth, I would reap (continuation in Chapter Four).

> Don't be misled—you cannot mock the justice of God. You will always harvest what you plant.
>
> Galatians 6:7 NLT

One year and a half later, the ministry upgraded from a plaza suite to a grand church building. Of course, we rejoiced and gave thanks, but as time went on, the most committed parishioners began to come less and less. As the youngest adult in the ministry, I was shielded from a lot of things that manifested behind closed doors. I hardly ever knew what was going on, nor did I pay close enough attention to the signs. I will never forget the day the pastor called a leadership meeting and announced that we had to give up the building. In addition to the heart-wrenching truth that we could not afford the building anymore, the pastor also announced the discontinuation of the ministry altogether.

In so many words, I felt like I had just gone through a hard breakup. I felt dropped. I chose not to go to church for about a month after that meeting. The news of the failed church and the fallen pastor spread like wildfire around the city and social media. People all over began to slander him and spread rumors concerning his past. However, because of my loyalty to the man of God, I was ready to defend his honor because I honored the word of God.

> "Do not touch my chosen people and do not hurt my prophets."
>
> Psalms 105:15 NLT

But that became very conditional when some speculations were confirmed as true. The spirit of gossip had consumed me. Unfortunately, my perspective was skewed, and I completely resented him. I had no respect for him, and I began to regret my affiliation with the ministry. Although I was hurt, embarrassed, and unforgiving, God still revealed his perfect plan to me when he guided me to the new age church that healed my addiction and changed my life two months later.

Amid these events, I never grasped the fact that the church did not hurt me. I never identified the reality that the leader just disappointed me.

The leader may have been prideful, secretive, hypocritical, and even judgmental at times. He was not perfect, but neither were we. In order for me to have healed properly, I had to put my feelings in the proper perspective. I was not a victim of church hurt. I was disappointed by my expectations of people in the church.

Many times, we resent God's will in our lives because we don't see what he is doing, nor do we know the result of it. I realized that in order for me to find my new church home, I had to transition from the last one.

The will of God still prevailed. At the new ministry, I was able to achieve the very things that were prophesied to me at the previous ministry. The transition had to happen, not just for me, but for every believer that was affiliated because God loved us more than our positions. He cared for our growth and hearts more than our titles and platforms. So, if the way to our hearts was through the closing of a ministry, God saw that as a fair trade. Glory to his name!

> "My thoughts are nothing like your thoughts," says the Lord. "And my ways are far beyond anything you could imagine. For just as the heavens are higher than the earth, so my ways are higher than your ways and my thoughts higher than your thoughts."
>
> Isaiah 56:8-9 NLT

When we rely on God as our source and keep our focus on him, he will begin to unfold his perfect plan to us. It is never to harm us but to help us. Please understand that the church never hurt you — your expectations of people did. When we become open to God's purpose for our life, forgiveness, understanding, compassion, and grace will flood our hearts after the hurt. We have all fallen short of God's glory. We all are not perfect, but when we focus on the source who is perfect, he will make us perfect and complete. We will lack nothing.

REVELATION

Clarity comes when the sun shines through the rain, but first, the climate has to change. What clarity are you robbing yourself of because you choose not to change your environment or perspective?

Chapter Three

LORD, WHERE IS MY SPOUSE?

"The man who finds a wife finds a treasure, and receives favor from the Lord."

Proverbs 18:22 (NLT)

A fter recovering from a previous relationship and politely exiting an ongoing situation-ship (which is another story for another book), I decided to take some time to deal with myself without a man. As I went on this journey in search of my identity and purpose, I made it my business not to pursue anyone. I knew that Heaven was backing me up because even when I wanted to go back, God shut every door, locked the windows, built a fence around the property, and put a 'Beware of Dog' sign on the gate.

After four months, I felt amazing. I was walking into the new me, and excited about everything God had in store for me. I knew that I was ready to start dating again! At least I thought I was.

One weekend, God instructed me to go back to my hometown. As I settled there and dwelled in the secret place a.k.a took a bath, I was consumed by insecurity as I compared myself to what I saw on social media. I believed that because I did not look as beautiful as the women I saw or have the following they had, I was not good enough. My rejection flared and hit the roof. At that moment, I knew that I was not ready to be with anyone. Yet, immediately, in my insecurity, Holy Spirit started affirming me through the word of God.

"You are fearfully and wonderfully made."

"I knew you before you were formed in your mother's womb."

"I created every part of you that you think is imperfect and said that it was good!"

"You are beautiful in my eyes."

"Masterpiece!"

"Beloved!"

"Treasure!"

"You are mine, and I am yours."

The overwhelming affection that Holy Spirit gave me almost made me forget where I was. I thought to myself, "Holy Spirit, I am naked and vulnerable. Are you really having this talk with me right now?"

It was an affection that I had only expected to receive from my husband one day. I was shaken up, but not uncomfortable, because his peace manifested in the affirmations. For 30-45 minutes in that tub, God revealed himself to me as the lover of my soul. That is when it dawned on me that my pursuit of marriage had become my source for finding intimacy. I relied on the affection of my future spouse to determine what love was for me when God is love.

> *"But anyone who does not love does not know God, for God is love."*
>
> 1 John 4:8 (NLT)

The process of being found by a submitted man of God can be very tedious. Nonetheless, God revealed to me that if I submitted to him, I wouldn't have to focus on being found. In my submission, he would reveal me to the man he ordained to be my husband. God is so beautiful because through his intimacy that night, he showed me the characteristics of my husband. He gave me insight of who my husband would be — NOT what he would look like, but who he would be. He made this known, not for me to idolize it, but for me to be aware of it when he came. Holy Spirit can give us amazing guidance if we let him. We search for him to show us how to make money and how to deal with our families, but he also cares about our love life. The process of elimination in intentional dating becomes so much easier when we begin to seek the love of Holy Spirit.

We must fix our source from finding a spouse and being married at a certain age, to seeking the traits of God and fulfilling the purpose that he has placed inside of us. Once he becomes the source of our love and companionship, the spouse will come, BUT, will you be aware of it?

"For I am about to do something new. See, I have already begun! Do you not see it? I will make a pathway through the wilderness. I will create rivers in the dry wasteland."

Isaiah 43:19 (NLT)

Section Two

UP YOUR
SOURCE

Chapter Four

VALIDATION

"For those who exalt themselves will be humbled, and those who humble themselves will be exalted."

Luke 14:11 (NLT)

A s previously expressed in Chapter Two, I was the choir directer's granddaughter in my youth, so I am a singer at heart. I did not fully become confident in my gift until I got to college. Once I did, I rested in that confidence. I had no desire to improve my ability because I just knew that I was a good singer. I became complacent, and status and platforms became my source of validation — until the Lord humbled me.

"For those who exalt themselves will be humbled, and those who humble themselves will be exalted."

Luke 14:11 (NLT)

It was through humility that I was able to become a better person. That is one of the many characteristics that I love about God. He does not seek to harm us. Everything he does is to help us. It may hurt, but growth will never happen in a comfortable place.

Unfortunately, it was really hard to bounce back from the humiliation of being humbled by God. My self-esteem was damaged, and I questioned if singing would be in my future. Entering into my sophomore year of college, I joined the gospel choir and was appointed as the Chaplain. It was my job to start every rehearsal with prayer, praise, and worship. So I sang on and off campus with the school choir and church praise team WHILE I was still doing what I wanted to do in the world. Eventually, my disobedience caught up with me.

May 2017, one week before my old church closed its doors, I was also demoted from my position in the school choir. Naturally, the correlation of these events does not sound like a big deal. Spiritually, it hit me like a ton of bricks. I realized that the hand of God had left me. At that moment, I could have blamed the devil for all of it. However, I knew that this was all my doing.

I became very low in spirit and thought less of myself. In one week, I lost everything that gave me status and importance. I lost my 'identity.' Even after partnering with my new church home, it still took a great deal of time for my self-esteem to rebuild. It actually became worse before it got better. My insecurity flared once I noticed I was surrounded by so many successful and thriving people. I saw through the lens of my dysfunction instead of accepting my season of stillness, regaining strategy, and allowing God to process me. I immediately started to feel rejected, undervalued, overlooked, and unappreciated. I felt like I was not good enough to be used. Instead of seeing the opportunity to be submitted under higher leadership and trusting their judgment concerning me, I felt hopeless.

I was so eager to be used! I wanted to show everyone how good I was. Yet, I never stopped long enough to deal with the issues that blinded me from God's will. I wanted to be accepted by everyone, but I did not accept myself. Striving for the approval of man almost drove me insane. When drawing from the source of people-pleasing, disappointment will always follow. It was not until I started living for God and pursuing the things of God that my mindset began to shift. I stopped viewing life through self-destruction and realized the lesson in it all. I am God's property first!

You are God's property first! He is your validation. When he takes up that space in your heart, you will not need another compliment from anyone else. You are gifted, wise, anointed, and appointed for such a time as this! Identity comes by first knowing who God is. Once that revelation is obtained, you will realize who you are! Your position, status, role, or job is NOT who you are; it's what you do. If those things were stripped from you today, who would you be? I came to the resolve that if I could not sing another tune for the rest of my life, I would still be Christ's servant. That is who I am. Who are you?

> "Obviously, I'm not trying to win the approval of people, but of God. If pleasing people were my goal, I would not be Christ's servant."
>
> Galatians 1:10 (NLT)

Chapter Five

REJECTION

"He was despised and rejected by mankind, a man of suffering, and familiar with pain. Like one from whom people hide their faces he was despised, and we held him in low esteem."

Isaiah 53:3 (NIV)

Believe it or not, I was completely oblivious to the spirit of rejection until I hit the age of 21. My pastor taught a series about rejection for a month. Throughout the beginning of the series, I kept thinking to myself, "Wow! I am so glad that is not me. That is crazy!" Yet the joke was on me. I soon came into the rude awakening that I had struggled with rejection for the majority of my life.

The day after my graduation from college, I had breakfast with my mother and grandmother. As we ate, my grandmother began to share the past of my late grandfather. He grew up in an environment that never showed him the love he needed as a child. So, when he met my grandmother, and they had children, he couldn't love them past the extent of the love he had experienced in his youth. The rejection that rested in my grandfather was now being passed down to my mother.

My mother and father always made sure their children were taken care of. I did not grow up in a broken home, nor was I neglected. Both of my parents loved me immensely. So, how did rejection still manifest in my life, if not through direct family issues? Throughout my school days, I was a pretty smart girl — Honor Roll, Dean's List, Honor Society, Enrichment, you name it. Despite my achievements, I was a mere outcast in the eyes of some of my peers. I am not going to glamorize this story by saying that I was always the victim and everyone was against me because it would not be true. I did not always make the right decisions. I did not always hang around the right people.

Approaching my 4th-grade year, my parents decided to move from the south side of town to the north. I had to adjust to a brand new environment, brand new school, and brand new faces. I was often pushed away because I was different.

"Go back to where you came from!"

"Why do you talk white?"

"I just don't like you."

"Go away. Leave me alone."

It all threw me for a loop. I had never felt so alienated before. No one told me how cruel kids could be, and I surely did not know how to retaliate. So I didn't say anything. I became very passive and socially awkward.

I believe the enemy tried to strip me of my self-esteem, confidence, and worth in those years, so I would not see myself as anything greater than that in the years to come. I was betrayed, denied, rejected, talked about, lied on, and bullied before the age of 13. I came to the resolution that if no one liked me for who I was, maybe they would like me for who I pretended to be. In an attempt to gain friendship with anybody, I created a new Kierston. Through the remaking of myself, I gained a few friends and became popular with some people. By the time I got to high school, I was apart of the band and lost about 10-20 pounds.

But, my efforts still were not good enough. People that I considered my closest friends denied me to their cliques, gave me a false sense of belonging, and ultimately kept me out of the loop concerning anything. I just could not fit in. I wanted so badly to be popular and accepted, that I became the very thing that I was experiencing — rejection. Chasing a popular crowd, I rejected so many genuine relationships and chased after the acceptance of the popular kids who rated me as lame, stupid, and nerdy. I regretted my decision so much that I carried that weight all through college.

At the age of 22, God removed the scales from my eyes. I no longer aspired to be something that everyone would like, but I focused on being the unapologetic one who God adored! That was the person that people ended up accepting. The authentic Kierston. With God as Lord over my life, I wanted him so much more than the acceptance of people.

When I made that decision, genuine relationships and divine connections began to find me. I did not have to chase anything else from that point on, and I did not have to live in rejection. I finally knew who I was. Once I increased my seek of God and up'd my source, he revealed identity to me!

Key Traits of Rejection:
- *Fabricated Personalities*
- *Tendency to reject others, so you are not the first to be rejected*
- *Opinionated Personality; desire to be included in every encounter or conversation*

Are You Struggling With The Spirit of Rejection?
-Pastor Adrian Davis

Chapter Six

"GOD KNOWS MY HEART"

"A good man produces good things from the treasury of a good heart, and an evil person produces evil things from the treasury of an evil heart. What you say flows from what is in your heart."

Luke 6:45 (NLT)

For quite some time, I tended to mask my judgments or intentions with the common phrase, "God knows my heart." In Luke, it declares that out of the abundance of our hearts, our mouths will reveal our true intent. So, if we proclaim that God still knows our hearts, it could still very well mean that based on our heart posture, what we say or how we treat others is an exact reflection of our heart. Over the years, I had to be very careful about what I allowed to get into my heart; TV shows, movies, relationships, and social media. They all aid in an unhealthy heart posture and will begin to fill us with darkness.

"Don't be fooled by those who say such things for bad company corrupts good character."

1 Corinthians 15:33 (NLT)

REVELATION

You committed to eating healthier this week, but the days got away from you, so you just ate what was convenient. Imagine eating all of your favorite foods. You devour some pizza, ice

37

cream, candy, etc. After a while, you feel sick. So you go to your nutritionist and say, "I wanted to eat better, but you know my intentions." However, he never knew your intentions. He knew what you did and saw what you ate. Now what you have consumed has made you ill.

Binge-watching Netflix is making you sick. Smoking is making you sick. Gossiping is making you sick! All of these things are liable to make our hearts unhealthy. We come to God expecting him to 'know our hearts' and excuse us when he sees the true intents of our hearts. We expect him to understand our intentions behind the things that we release, but we were never intentional about the very things that we consumed.

> "You are the light of the world. A town built on a hill cannot be hidden. Neither do people light a lamp and put it under a bowl. Instead they put it on its stand, and it gives light to everyone in the house. In the same way, let your light shine before others, that they see your goods and glorify your Father in heaven."
>
> Matthew 5:14-16 (NIV)

Chapter Seven

FASTING

"...where he {Jesus} was tempted by the devil for forty days. Jesus ate nothing all that time and became very hungry. Then the devil said to him,"If you are the son of God tell this stone to become a loaf of bread." but Jesus told him, "No! The Scriptures say. 'People do not live by bread alone.'"

Luke 4:2-4 (NLT)

W e are so funny. We always expect God to do things for us simply because we asked him to. We want him to heal our broken hearts, deliver us from temptation, lead us to our spouses, and allow us to become successful overnight, all because these are 'the desires of our hearts.' Now, I am not saying that there is anything wrong with asking God for what we want. However, I do find it strange that we ask for things but do not position ourselves to receive it. God actually wants us to acquire these things! But because we do not position ourselves and up our source to hear his instructions, we fall subject to our own will being done and not his.

REVELATION

When fasting, we are working out our spiritual muscles, very similar to working out our actual muscles. Our flesh is the spiritual fat we have allowed ourselves to gain over time (soulties, relationships, greed, pride, lying, cursing, gossip, etc.) This fat is the dead weight we harbor around for the sake of feeling good, having fun, or relaxing.

As we begin to fast from these things (or fast in general), our spirit begins to take up the space that our flesh once consumed. Denying the things that our flesh loves makes our spirit stronger and allows us to make better decisions for our future. Once we exercise the principle of fasting long enough, the soreness will fade, and our spiritual muscles will be revealed — how much wiser, focused, determined, submitted, and better we are. Yet, the catch is, we have to keep it up, so we don't gain that dead weight again.

Fasting is literally the second fastest way that I have found to receive wisdom, strategy, revelation, and reflection from God. The Bible is the first. Initially, I hated fasting because I loved food. So, in reality, I chose food over God. I ate for comfort, stress relief, and many other life issues. Food was physical. Drinking was easily accessible. Pornography was at my fingertips. I knew all of these things were here in the earth that could be a quick fix, but it was only through fasting that God began to give me insight and wisdom on what I could be doing differently with less damage to myself (spiritually, mentally, emotionally, and physically).

Through fasting, we allow God to deal with the most vulnerable parts of ourselves that we would never want anyone else to see. As the source of our comfort, God causes even the most obscene things in our lives to work for our good. He desires us to live in abundance and be healed from our afflictions. It would be pointless to give us all of these wonderful things while we have the same detrimental mindsets that cause us to repeat the dysfunctional cycles. Fasting is a way to sober ourselves and renew our minds in order for us to be ready for the things that we desire most to advance the kingdom.

> "And we know that God causes everything to work together for the good of those who love God and are called according to his purpose for them."
>
> Romans 8:28 (NLT)

> "You intended to harm me, but God intended it all for good. He brought me to this position so I could save the lives of many people."
>
> Genesis 50:20 (NLT)

Section Three

WHY THE
SOURCE

Chapter Eight

THE CORRECTION

"For the Lord disciplines and corrects those whom he loves, and he punishes every son whom he receives and welcomes {to his heart}."

Hebrews 12:6 (AMP)

Let's backtrack to chapter two for one second. Remember the sentence that referred to me 'doing my own thing' and still serving in ministry? Good, because what I am about to share reflected God's correction in this portion of my life. Ready? I'm not...

It was my freshman year in college. Later that February, I began dating this guy (which is another story for another book). We, in turn, dated for two years, living our best lives together — outside of the will of God. Approaching the last months of our relationship, God began speaking to me in my dreams. Every other night, I would wake up disturbed at the memory of him and me arguing. It would be the same arguments but different scenarios. Unfortunately, I knew God was trying to tell me that our relationship was not going to last any longer. One year before the dreams, my pastor at the time randomly called me down to the altar one service and spoke three words that ruined my life,

"Let it go."

In so many words, I manifested horribly. I had never fought

God so hard on anything, but when he commanded this of me, something in me would not allow it. I had no idea why I did not want to let the relationship go. Although I knew I had to, I still tried to make it work and somehow convince God to change his mind about us parting ways. After I made it clear to God that I was not going to let my boyfriend go, he decided to take the relationship from me instead. I will never forget it.

I was in my prayer closet, making a list of things that my boyfriend and I would accomplish together. I felt so good about it! I finally felt that things were going to be okay. Oh, but when I came out of that closet, all of hell broke loose in my relationship. We got into another argument that drew the last straw on his patience. Just like that, we broke up for good. God harshly revealed to me that he could not go where I was going. Over the next year of singleness, God began to deal with ME. All of my self-esteem, bad habits, trust issues, rejection, lust, pride, and manipulation problems. I was really crazy, but I would not have known that until God, the Source, revealed himself to me as 'The Corrector' who loves me. His correction saved my life and taught me a valuable lesson. God will never withhold anything from me that is good for me, so I had to trust that. In hindsight, the relationship was not good for me, and God's correction protected me.

Just think about it, we all would be out in this world aimless and confused, living in distress and dysfunction, not knowing what our purpose would be if it had not been for God's correction on us.

Rebuke:
an expression of sharp disapproval or criticism.

As I was in the midst of silent prayer, a memory of my first rebuke manifested. So many thoughts ran through my mind. I thought about how offended I was. I felt discouraged. I wondered why God hardly had anything good to say about me and why he chose — in the middle church of all places — to cast the rebuke. However, in my silent prayer, God began to show me the perspective that I missed in it all.

REVELATION

"What would you rather I say? Marriage, promotion, money, healing? What if the way to those things was through my correction? I understand. You do not always want to hear what you are doing wrong or where you are flawed. Yet, how do you expect to become better? The real privilege is in the rebuke, not the blessing. You always ask my prophets, 'What is the Lord saying?' but you cringe when you receive your answer. I know you can sing, act, write, draw, speak well, dance, and all of these other things. I created you.

Nonetheless, what is the use of an amazing singer, accurate prophet, anointed intercessor, or phenomenal artist if their hearts are not right? You evangelize so well, but your soul is on the fence. I will not allow it. So do not let the spirit of offense swell within you. I love you too much for you to remain the same. Do not rebel out of your promise because my correction was inconvenient."

-God

Chapter Nine

HOLY SPIRIT

"So you have not received a spirit that makes you fearful slaves. Instead, you received God's Spirit when he adopted you as his own children. Now we call him, "Abba, Father." For his Spirit joins with our spirit to affirm that we are God's children."

Romans 8:15-16 (NLT)

First of all, I would like to declare publicly: HOLY SPIRIT IS MY BEST FRIEND. That is all. Growing up in a Baptist denomination, entities like Holy Spirit were very mystical to the youth. The elders always got excited at the mention of his power, and the children were left settling in the dust of religion and traditionalism because of our lack of understanding. I used to think that the Holy Ghost was an actual ghost — a creature that floated around in the room and haunted us.

My entire life and perspective of who God was changed in early 2018. My church was placed on an assignment to read, 'Good Morning, Holy Spirit' by Benny Hinn. A few chapters in, I stood in amazement of the relationship that Hinn had with Holy Spirit. I wanted that kind of relationship too! I officially accepted Holy Spirit into my life at the age of 22, and I cannot fathom how I managed to navigate through life before then.

The initial experience was not overwhelming. There was no crowd of people. I did not roll around on the floor speaking in tongues, or feel fire 'shut up in my bones.' I remember lying in my bed, falling onto my knees, and uttering these words:

"Holy Spirit, I acknowledge that you are real, and I accept your presence in my life to guide and direct my steps." It was rather quiet at first. I sat on the floor in total silence.

Nonetheless, in that silence, I received a revelation. God took me back to when I was 12 years old. I was sitting in the same spot in the middle of my bedroom floor, talking to my imaginary friend. We didn't speak or hang out anymore because of my growth into adolescence and my desire for human companionship. At that moment, I realized that my imaginary friend was the Holy Spirit the entire time. That period of my life was the last time that I had ever embraced him, and in a matter of minutes, I was right back where we left off. This revelation of my childhood imaginary friend blew my mind! I had a brand new perspective of the Holy Spirit. After getting to know him, I noticed that he was an actual person with feelings, thoughts, and truths. He is a lover, comforter, and gentleman. It was after I understood him that I began to love him and truly receive him.

It was so crazy. I would start crying randomly during prayer. I began to weep uncontrollably at the partaking of communion. I prayed for people that I did not like. I had unsettling feelings at random moments. I felt more convicted than usual. They were never fearful convictions, but rather nurturing convictions that spoke volumes to my heart. Holy Spirit believed that I could be a better person, and he walked with me the entire way. Knowing this about him made me want to be better, not just for me, but because he was a part of me. He is literally my best friend!

Holy Spirit is assigned to each of our lives as our helper since Jesus is now rightfully seated next to our Father in heaven. It is through his help that we all can learn how to handle our struggles and overcome our curses. Being connected to Holy

Spirit gives us a direct line to the heart and mind of God.

> "And I will ask the Father and He will give you another Helper (Comforter, Advocate, Intercessor, Counselor, Strengthener, Standby), to be with you forever."
>
> John 14:16 (AMP)

Yes, this revelation of Holy Spirit amazed me, but it took a while for me to grow confident in actually hearing the voice of God. For months, I over-analyzed everything. It was hard to decipher my thoughts from his. I became frustrated because there was a required level of discipline that I had not yet tapped into. So, I gained an understanding of what I sought after. I started studying the Holy Bible. I read about Holy Spirit, Jesus, the parables of Jesus, the Disciples, obtaining wisdom, the authority of those who receive Holy Spirit and wisdom, etc. Once I understood the language of God, I began to comprehend the dialogue between us.

It's impossible to travel to a foreign land with no knowledge of their language or culture and expect to understand them. This is how many of us have been approaching God. We talk to him on occasion, and since we do not get an understanding of his language, we feel alone and disconnected from him. But just like in every earthly profession, it takes knowledge and training to operate at one's fullest potential.

I had to keep reading his word because everything in the Bible was originated through his Spirit. I also conversed with him every day. I was so desperate to hear God's voice that I committed to pray every morning before I fiddled with my phone or talked to anyone. My prayer life was very unsatisfactory prior to this decision, so it amazed me to see how this small change made such an impact on my life. My thoughts began to change. I stopped hanging around certain people. I let go of some relationships that I previously did not have the strength to release. Prayer gave me perspective, and Holy Spirit, my best friend, guided me. All I needed was the faith to be obedient to God's voice and the knowledge of God's word to confirm what was said.

> *"So faith comes from hearing, that is, hearing the Good News about Christ."*
>
> Romans 10:17 (NLT)

> *"My sheep listen to my voice; I know them, and they follow me."*
> John 10:27 (NLT)

When we allow God room in our lives to be our source, Holy Spirit will begin to reveal marvelous things to us! Trust Holy Spirit. He is here for us, and he is the closest connection we can ever have to God until the day of Christ's return. He gives us the insight to become whom God has always intended for us to be. But he will not force his way into our hearts. Holy Spirit is a lover, not a fighter. My prayer is that he becomes all of these things and more to you.

UNDERSTANDING THE VOICE OF GOD

Everything you receive from Holy Spirit should be supported by scripture. There are three voices in your head at all times: God's, yours, and the devil's. It is vital to fast, study, and pray so that our spirits may be filled, and familiar with the things of God. By doing this, the voice of God becomes clear, and we gain the strength to silence the enemy's lies in our heads.

Chapter Ten

THE GRACE IN OBEDIENCE

"But Samuel replied, 'What is more pleasing to the Lord: your burnt offerings and sacrifices or your obedience to his voice? Listen! Obedience is better than sacrifice, and submission is better than offering the fat of rams.'"

1 Samuel 15:22 (NLT)

Has God ever instructed you to do something, but you did not understand it? Welcome to the club! "The Lord works in mysterious ways." is not just a common phrase. Trusting the voice of God is always an act of faith. However, obeying the voice of God certainly exceeds that level of faith.

> "As Jesus and the disciples left the town of Jericho, a large crowd followed behind. Two blind men were sitting beside the road. When they heard that Jesus was coming that way, they began shouting, "Lord, Son of David, have mercy on us!" "Be quiet!" the crowd yelled at them. But they only shouted louder, "Lord, Son of David, have mercy on us!" When Jesus heard them, he stopped and called, "What do you want me to do for you?" "Lord," they said,"we want to see!" Jesus felt sorry for them and touched their eyes. Instantly they could see! Then they followed him."
>
> Matthew 20:29-34 (NLT)

The blind men had enough faith to follow Jesus. They called to him even though they could not see. Everyone around them saw them as foolish men. BUT GOD! He honored their persistence and granted them their sight. The most pivotal part of this passage, for me, was not the miracle. It was their pursuit after the miracle. There were many times that I received miracles from God, worshiped the miracle, and left his presence. Since I placed God back on the throne of my heart, my pursuit for him surpassed the miracles that he performed. This allowed me to be far more spiritually flexible with my obedience to his voice.

There are moments when I get stuck in my tracks concerning my faith, because I could not see what my life would be beyond the voice that I was obeying. Yet through his pursuit of me, God changed my spiritual sight and revealed something even more valuable to my life than presents.

I was in prayer one morning, and I heard God say very clearly, "Go home." My home was three hours away! I was very confused and unsure because I could barely afford the gas to make it home and back, but I was obedient. I didn't pack any clothes or let anyone know that I was coming. When I arrived, I met my dad in the driveway. Excited, he asked why I was there. In complete confidence, I said, "I don't know." Shortly after getting settled in, my father exclaimed how relieved he was that I caught the family before they traveled to my grandmother's house (which was another 3-hour drive in a different direction). I immediately assumed that this was the reason why God told me to get home.

The next day, we went to my grandmother's house. It was a wonderful, refreshing time. In the midst of our conversation, I decided to ask, "Grandma, have you been praying that I would come and visit you soon?"

With a subtle grin, she replied, "Yes."

I was so excited! I followed the voice of God, but it was for my grandmother! The trip had nothing to do with me receiving anything in particular, but it had everything to do with God answering someone else's prayer through me.

He allowed me the grace to be a blessing to someone else simply through my obedience. The experience was so enriching. It taught me that even when I get caught up in my own life, I should always be looking for ways to be a blessing to others. For this, I was grateful.

Although it may be scary, I admonish you to trust God and allow his perfect plan to unfold. He did not give us the spirit of fear because it forfeits our ability to try! I encourage you to try God and watch him blow your mind all because of your obedience to his voice.

> "For God has not given us the spirit of fear and timidity, but of power, love, and self-discipline."
>
> 2 Timothy 1:7 (NLT)

━━━━━ Chapter Eleven ━━━━━

COURAGE TO DO IT SCARED

"This is my command - Be strong and courageous! Do not be afraid or discouraged. For the Lord your God is with you wherever you go."
Joshua 1:9 (NLT)

When I was between the ages of 12-14, I tapped into various creative heights. At home, school, and friends' houses, I always had a bright idea about something. I drew pictures, wrote scripts, made up cartoon and drama series, created songs, formed musical groups, choreographed dance routines, and sketched witty inventions. On a scale from 1-10, my ambition ranked at 11.5. By the time I got to high school, my determination had declined to a solid five because of the season I had endured in the years prior. I joined the band, and there is where my aspirations thrived once more for the next four years.

I worked hard to prove myself worthy of my position. Every day in the scorching heat and every night in the cold, I put everything I had into that part of my life. I reaped the fruits of my labor the very next year when I became the captain of the flag team. There was a price I had to pay for excellence -- discipline. I battled intense anxiety. I always anticipated the hardships that would come with the territory: slander, gossip, betrayal, the pressure to deliver, and temptation of every kind.

Sometimes, I wanted to give up and throw the whole opportunity away. Still, in the midst of it all, everything I endured established the character of who I am today. Determination, resilience, discipline, patience, focus, and perspective were birthed from the pressures of my life. I was scared to lead, but because God was my source, even back then, he gave me the courage to do it scared.

As the years went by, and I advanced to my senior year in college, I decided to join a campus organization. To move forward into the membership process, I had to prove myself worthy of representing the institution. There were rules I had to follow and information I had to learn in my free time. In my pursuit of this organization, I still had to uphold my commitment to my studies and school work. It challenged me at a greater capacity than what I was used to. Many days I wanted to walk away, but because I wanted to be a part, and was invested in the process, I persevered and earned my membership.

In late 2018, God placed a burden on my heart for the needs of his people, and I did not want to do it. I was inexperienced and unqualified for what God was asking of me. In the midst of my insecurity, he said,

> "You were also unqualified to lead a squad, but you did. You were also too inexperienced to be a part of that organization, but now you are. You wanted these things! You worked hard, studied, and showed yourself approved. You did these things for you. You did these things without me. Now imagine how much you could accomplish now that you have me! Imagine how much farther you could go in my name! Yes, you are not doing this for you. But can you do it for the one who created you?"

When I was obedient to his will, he granted me the grace to do it while afraid. At a very stressful time in my life, God reminded me of those two events. There were times when I want to give up on the assignment. But God had to show me that wherever there is fear, there is no room for him to perform. My faith and fear could not live together. So I chose faith, thus choosing God as my source.

Fear will happen, but it is our responsibility to overcome it. God has called us to conquer great mountains and kill mighty giants. Unfortunately, instead of living up to God's expectations of us, we cower in the name of fear when he has already graced us for victory. God will use the least expected things to spark a great change in the earth. How will you act when that great change is you? How will you respond when the assignment on your life has the capability to shake the very foundations of the world? God desires to carry us from faith to faith and glory to glory, but we cannot get stagnant and grow weary because all we can see is the mountain. God will never bring us so far in our faith just to leave us in the face of adversity. Instead, he gives us the courage to keep moving even when we cannot see the Promised Land yet. He knows what we can do and handle. We have to trust him as our source and rely on him to provide what we cannot. Do it scared! The world is waiting for what God has placed inside of you.

Chapter Twelve

FAVOR FINDS THE FAITHFUL

"So do not throw away this confident trust in the Lord. Remember the great reward it brings you!"

Hebrews 10:35 (NLT)

February 2018, God told me to quit my job. I was finishing out my senior year of college and trying to keep my head above water. I was terrified, but I was obedient (after a couple of days). I wrote my resignation letter and worked my last two weeks. I immediately started contemplating if I made the right decision. I prayed for a sign, and on my last payday, God blessed my bank account with ten times more than what I worked for!

I was elated about what God had done, but the celebration came to a screeching halt the week of finals and exit exams for the graduating seniors. I was scrambling to keep my 3.6 GPA and my sanity. The year had been stressful, and now I didn't have a job. Nonetheless, I held my head high and placed my focus on the source. I chose to stop worrying about tomorrow and make the best out of every moment.

I had to leave town due to ministry obligations for the university and returned after the commencement of finals, so I missed my first final exam of the week. Fresh off the bus, I rushed over to my professor's office to inquire about my exam. I took a seat, and he asked me, "Why do you have a C in my class, Ms. Lewis?"

I froze. "I have no idea, Doc." I replied in shock and exhaustion, "I've studied the material, and I've done the homework."

He continued to interrogate me concerning my plans after college. I had none. After making that confession, he grew frustrated and began scolding me about how irresponsible I was being.

In an attempt to hold back as many tears as possible, I proclaimed with as much boldness and energy that I had left, "I don't have a plan, sir, but I have enough faith to know that since God has brought me through college, he will provide for me after college."

He paused. We sat in silence until he received a phone call. Meanwhile, I was still holding my tears.

After he finished the phone call, he said to me, "I have a graduation gift for you. You have an A in my class. You do not have to take the final, and you are free from attending the rest of the classes."

At this point, I was drowning in my tears. Not only did God bless me financially, but he allowed favor to hit my academics. Before I left his office that day, he expressed to me, " Just continue to be a great person, impact the world, and change lives."

I could go on and on about how God favored me after graduating from college, but I will settle here and say that when we give God access to our lives, we permit him to do whatever he wants to do. I choose not to believe that these things occurred by coincidence — it was the grace of God! I decided not to worry about my situation, gave it ALL to the source, and he exceeded my expectations! I trusted God with all of me, and he revealed to me everything that he always intended for me — nothing missing or lacking.

You may ask, "Why should I make God the source of my life?" My question to you is, "Why not?" Why not give all of your cares to someone who actually wants them?

> *"Give all your worries and cares to God, for he cares about you."*
> 1 Peter 5:7 (NLT)

Why not commit your life to someone who can do more with it than you ever could?

> *"For I know the plans I have for you," says the Lord. "They are plans for good and not for disaster, to give you a future and a hope."*
> Jeremiah 29:11 (NLT)

Why not submit to someone who truly loves, forgives, and desires nothing but the best for your life?

> *"The thief's purpose is to steal and kill and destroy. My purpose is to give them a rich and satisfying life."*
> John 10:10 (NLT)

God can heal you from your pain, deliver you from your past, and bless you beyond your imagination. He can do all of these things for you, but he needs your heart. He needs access to you so he can give you exactly what he intends for you. Will you be faithful to him as your source so that his favor can find you?

Section Four

RESOURCES

FROM THE AUTHOR

Through all of these things, I never neglected the fact that freedom is a process. So I admonish you! Do not discount what God is doing concerning your healing. Instead, keep moving forward and know that the battle is already won! Yes, you messed up, but God has more grace for you than you have sin. I pray that my experiences, mistakes, struggles, trials, and tribulations were able to help you in your walk with The Source. Keep drawing to God, and he will draw close to you. God Bless You.

TO RECEIVE CHRIST

If you have no idea who this God is that I speak of and you made it to this point in the book, I believe you want to know the true source of everything that we ever need. If you desire to receive Jesus Christ as your Lord and Savior, all you have to do is openly declare that Jesus is Lord and believe in your heart that God raised him from the dead. You will be saved and gain access to the abundant life he has for you.

"For it is by believing in your heart that you are made right with God, and it is by openly declaring your faith that you are saved."
Romans 10:9-10 (NLT)

Congratulations! You have just made
the best decision of your life.

TALK TO THE SOURCE

Prayer is how we communicate with God. It's not just something we do when life is hard. Prayer should be something we do daily. Nevertheless, there are times when we feel the need to pray more. Sometimes, we endure trials and tribulations so intense that we don't know how or where to begin the conversation with God. Below are a few prayer starters for different topics. Use them to begin your conversation with God about the issues you may deal with.

ADDICTION

Dear God,

Thank you for covering me in my darkest hour and healing me from the inside out with the blood of Jesus. I openly profess with my mouth that I am no longer addicted to the things that my flesh craves, but I put my flesh and thoughts under subjection and pray that you begin to give me the strength to say, "No" and stay on the path that you have designed for me. Begin to place people in my life to hold me accountable. Show me the new life that awaits me in my future. I am not addicted, but I am free! Your word says that many are the afflictions of the righteous, but you will deliver us out of them all. So I believe by faith that you will.

In Jesus' Name. Amen.

CHURCH HURT

Father God,

I come before you in thankfulness. Thank you for seeing me through the trauma that I experienced. Thank you for allowing it to happen. Thank you for making me stronger through the challenges in life. I no longer hold on to the hurt from past leaders in the church, but I forgive them. I pray that you bless their lives and guide them to becoming even greater people for your glory. I pray that you begin to create a clean heart within me to look past their shortcomings. God, I pray for your healing and understanding to rest on me. I let go of the past pain of ministries and embrace the future that you have in store for me.

In Jesus' Name. Amen.

INTIMACY & COMPANIONSHIP

Heavenly Father,

Thank you for your unconditional love for me. I repent for the times I put marriage and relationship above you. I choose to put you back on the throne as my companion and lover. For you are love, God. I thank you for being patient with me and showing compassion towards me, even when I neglected you. Now God, reveal yourself to me in a new way. In every area of my life that I have trusted people to provide love and companionship, I now give it back to you. I am not lonely, because you said in your word that you would never leave nor forsake me. I trust you to send the spouse that you have for me in your timing. Give me the restraint to not idolize what is on the way. Thank you.

In Jesus' Name. Amen.

VALIDATION

Dear Lord God,

Thank you for delivering me from the opinions of people. Thank you for accepting me for everything that I am! Thank you for showing me who I am, even in the midst of trial and tribulation. God, I receive you as my validation. I declare that I am accepted by you. I come out of agreement with insecurity, and I come into agreement with who you say that I am. God, I thank you for calling me your friend, child, and servant. Heal every wound from my past and reveal your wonderful truths about me. I forgive those who rejected me and give you glory for the validation that you have already provided for me! I am not broken; I am whole! I am not bound; I am free! I am not lost; I am found! Thank you for giving me my identity back, and I decree all of these things to be so.

In Jesus' Name. Amen.

REJECTION

God,

Thank you for reminding me of how much you have accepted me as your child. Thank you for calling me your beloved masterpiece, treasure, and workmanship. I believe that since Jesus died for my rejection, I no longer have to live with it. Thank you for healing every infirmity in my heart that allowed me to reject good relationships and even greater accountability. Change my perspective to see the truth. I will no longer see from the lens of rejection, but I will be content in your truth. Give me the wisdom to guard my heart against any spirit that will push me out of your presence.

In Jesus' Name. Amen.

ENTITLEMENT

Lord God,

I repent for every time that I have taken your gifts for granted. I repent for dwelling in the spirit of entitlement. I wish to be humble in the face of opportunity, God. Thank you for giving me humility. Protect me from my selfish ambition.

I am grateful for everything that you have blessed me with, and I am thankful for everything you blocked to protect me. I repent for putting my position, status, and role above you. I place you back in your rightful place. It was never by my efforts but of your grace and mercy that I made it this far. I give you all of the glory, honor, and praise.

In Jesus' Name. Amen.

FASTING

Dear Heavenly Father,

Thank you for giving me an understanding of your principles. I pray that you will begin to take my willingness to fast to another level. God, I desire to hear you clearer than ever before. I no longer want to be in limbo between the voices of yours, mine, and the enemy. I desire your direction for my life, Lord. Give me deeper revelations of you in my moments of fasting. I pray that my worship begins to reach greater heights. Trust me with your voice. I desire to see your perfect plan. I long to be used by you in every capacity! God, enlarge my territory that I may have more room for you.

In Jesus' Name. Amen.

CORRECTION

Dear Father,

Thank you for correcting me because you love me. Thank you for allowing your rebuke to redefine who I am. Thank you for redirecting my steps back to the path that you designed for me. I do not desire to be outside of your will. Thank you for the leaders you have placed in my life to give language for my future. I release the spirit of offense and bind myself to your understanding. For your word says that in all things, we should get an understanding. Give me greater understanding. Introduce me to your wisdom. May your word resound loud in my ear to receive the correction that is needed to enhance my future. Thank you, Lord!

In Jesus' Name. Amen.

RELATIONSHIP WITH HOLY SPIRIT

Lord Jesus,

Thank you for your commission here on earth to redirect our lives forever. Even more, thank you for not leaving us here alone. I thank you for sending the helper, comforter, friend, counselor, and corrector that we know to be Holy Spirit. I receive Holy Spirit as my guide. I pray that our relationship grows stronger. I will not dismiss or reject him, but I will embrace him! Holy Spirit, thank you for being patient with me and remaining in my life. You are gentle, kind, and loving. I pray that our bond may never be separated. I rebuke every attack of the enemy that would steer me from your presence, and I declare that you are seated on the throne of my life.

In Jesus' Name. Amen.

GRACE

God,

Thank you for your grace and mercy that has covered me thus far. Thank you for giving me the grace to do the difficult things. I thank you that in every struggle, there is strength. Thank you for being my strength when I am weak. Thank you for gracing me to stand even when I was on the brink of falling. It is by your grace that I am not consumed with the cares of life. Your grace covers my shortcomings! Now, God, I ask that you continue to show me your manifested grace here in the earth. Remind me of your grace when life becomes hard. Remind me of your grace when my faith grows weary. Remind me of your grace when I feel that this mountain will never move. Remind me of your grace when I want to give up! I need your grace. Please, Lord, never let it depart from me.

In Jesus' Name. Amen.

FEAR

Father,

Thank you for not giving me the spirit of fear. I choose to walk in love, peace, and self-control. I understand that where fear is present, faith is not. Give me more faith than the enemy has given me fear. I will no longer fear failure! I will not lose my confident trust in you, Lord! For it is in you that we have victory over fear. I decree that fear is under my feet, and I will walk boldly into my future. Fear no longer lives here. God, I place you back in my heart where you belong. Fear will no longer direct me, but faith will!

In Jesus' Name. Amen.

FAVOR

God,

Thank you for favoring me. I do not take your favor for granted, and I thank you for allowing it to manifest in my life. I pray that you begin to use me as a beacon of light to people in my community. Send favor to my house, in the banks, classrooms, jails, courthouses, barbershops, salons, and grocery stores. Allow your favor to impact my job, business, ministry, school, church, house, and my dedication to you. I desire to be blessed and bear witness to those who are wavering in their faith. I pray that you grant me favor with the government, senate, president, military, and beneficiaries! Grant me your favor and keep me from misusing it! Allow me access to remind the world that you still perform MIRACLES, SIGNS, and WONDERS. Allow your favor to find the faithful.

In Jesus' Name. Amen.

ABOUT THE AUTHOR

Born and raised in Selma, Alabama, Kierston Lewis is a young, future-focused leader who loves shining light on the tough topics of life. She is currently a partner of All Nations Worship Assembly-Huntsville, where she serves as a leader in the Partner Services Department and sings with the Praise and Worship Team.

Lewis is a recent graduate of Alabama A&M University, where she received her Bachelor of Arts in Psychology and is now pursuing her Masters in Human Service Counseling in Christian Ministries. She enjoys singing praise and worship at her local assembly and traveling to new places. Lewis also enjoys quiet mornings in the park and spontaneous evening events that promote self-care. Most of all, Kierston Lewis loves to serve. Wherever there is a need, she always maintains a posture that helps bring the vision to life.

"I don't even like to read a book, let alone write one!" Those were the exact words of Kierston Lewis in 2016 when the Lord revealed that she would soon become an author. Although she never thought publishing a book would be in her future, Lewis believes that because she was willing and obedient, God's heart will be heard through the pages and between the lines which will lead others to Christ.

Her advice for writers young and old is to be reminded that

their stories are waiting to be heard.

"If you are called to write it, that makes you credible. No matter how over-saturated the market looks, there will always be room for the obedient."

STAY CONNECTED

Thank you for reading, *The Source*. Kierston looks forward to connecting with you and keeping you updated on her next releases. Below are a few ways you can connect with the author.

FACEBOOK Kierston S. Lewis
INSTAGRAM iam_kierston
EMAIL kierston.lewis@gmail.com